How To Overcome Financial
Problems And Improve Finances

Table of Contents

Financial Problems Are Just Part of Life

We all should spend our life with positivist. No matter what the situation is, keeping the focus intact is extremely important. We should have an aim to achieve because it determines the constancy of our life. There are many aspects of a human's existence such as social, financial, political and much more. But considering the larger impact, the financial aspect is more crucial than any other. If we are financially satisfied, we can ensure a better life for us.

We study hard to have a superior professional life and while working in an organization, we work hard to make sure a smooth living of our family. Regular monthly income has actually controlled our financial life because we can have a settled family budget. Fulfilling all the regular financial activities is not the problem for us. Such activities can be buying goods, paying utility bills, medical bills, education fees, etc.

A continuous monthly income source allows us to keep the finances intact. But, the problems start coming when we are no longer employed. Reasons can be many of leaving the job, but unemployment certainly invites a number of problems for us. With no arrival of regular income, our entire monthly budget gets disturbed and winning over the sudden expenses is almost impossible.

Getting over such serious problem and that would be on immediate basis becomes our priority. At first step, we would approach our friends or relatives to have some money. They definitely help with few funds, but the problem continues if Wait of getting new employment goes longer. In such scenario, applying for the loan comes as the last option for us. A loan is a useful financial tool that provides necessary funds during the adverse period of our financial life.

Solutions are available for your financial crisis

When losing the employment and no other source of income, we generally feel alone and hesitate to make our acquaintances familiar with our worse financial condition. But our perception change when we see that the loan companies are all set to help us with effective loan options.

It all depends upon us how we understand the importance of loans? The reality is that we should know loans are the only financial source to secure funds without any difficulty. Looking for the loans becomes more intrinsic when lenders are available at the marketplace with a wide range of loans, such as unemployed loans, Long term loans, no guarantor loans, etc. These types of loans are generally dedicated for the jobless individuals or those, who are trapped into rigorous financial problems.

Borrowing funds was not as easy as the Modern day lenders providing at the moment. We are not just anticipating it; in fact, it is a reality because traditional lenders were extremely specific when providing funds to those, who did not have a financial credibility. For instance, people with bad credit score do not have any integrity to show because they already have a poor credit record. How can a bank or a lender believe on these individuals? These lenders have every right to get back their funds within the time schedule.

Such restrictions on the borrowers are practical at the marketplace, but there is another reality too. Nowadays, whether they are unemployed or have a bad credit score, lenders have the provision of assisting financially to them. Therefore, solutions are available now for every financial problem.

Right use of the loans is mandatory

The flexible lending approach of the lenders paves the way for feasible financial aids for a number of people. There are many individuals, facing the tough challenges of bad credit score, unemployment, medical emergency, increasing debts and much more. The presence of multiple loan options enables these individuals to apply for a loan that fix to their financial requirements.

Getting a loan has also become easy because the lenders are ready to accept the loan applications of the people without any guarantor. While searching out the marketplace, you will experience that many credit lenders are providing loans without guarantor and that would be on affordable terms and conditions. Of course, lenders will not disburse large amount and they only offer small funds to borrow, but the loan applicants have the advantage of getting funds instantaneously thanks to the online procedure to submit the applications.

Availing funds is not a difficult task these days. But, lenders do not tolerate any kind of recklessness from the borrowers. Lenders are providing loans on variable terms, but they do not compromise with the wrong information given in the application form. True personal details ensure the chances of getting funds quickly.

Do Not Bother, When Financial Problems Are Hurting You

Hope such explanation is enough to describe that the financial problems are only the part of life. They will unsettle your life up to some extent, but not permanently. The existence of multiple loan options indicates that there is no lack of opportunities for the people. The crucial thing is that how an individual reacts to such funding opportunities.

Feeling worry during the unemployment or any other sort of financial crisis is natural. Still, there is no need to bother. Apply for loans, follow instructions sincerely and see how quickly you get desired financial outcomes in your life.

Where Do Your Financial Problems Come From?

Do you find yourself getting into debt and struggling with other financial problems? Are you one of the millions of Americans that is suffering during these hard economic times? If you answered yes, then this article is for you. Most importantly, now is the time to start taking care of these problems. By sitting back and doing nothing, then your problems will only begin to grow. But before you do this, you must identify where these problems began.

Most people's financial problems are the result of the idea of "buy now, pay later." Many people want the things their parents have, but rather than working hard and saving up for these things, they want them now. So, people buy on credit and think that they will just pay it off later. While our parents saved up and paid for most things in cash, we pull out our credit cards and don't take enough time to consider the consequences.

When you buy something on credit, another thing to be considered is that you not only have to eventually pay it off, but you also have to pay interest. Interest rates can get high and the longer it takes you to pay off your credit cards, the more the interest builds and the more you get into debt. So that television you bought on credit for $2000 ends up costing you $2600 instead. While that $2000 television is a fun thing to have, it has put you into debt and you are now a slave to the credit card company and they won't leave you alone until you have paid off your debt.

Another reason people struggle financially is that they do not take the time to sit down and write a budget. They don't manage their money wisely, so they end up spending more money than they make each month. You must take the time to sit down and figure out your monthly income and your monthly expenses. Once you have that figured out you can decide how much money to use each month to pay off debts and to put into savings.

Your financial problems come because you aren't managing your money and you are buying things you can't afford. Sit down and set some financial goals and create a plan on how you will get out of debt and put some extra money in the bank. Get rid of the idea of "buy now, pay later" and instead think in terms of "save now, buy later and avoid debt."

Common Financial Problems We All Face Everyday

There are three common financial problems that all humans face every day of their lot. They're actually much more than three, but we will go into three specific ones and depth throughout this article. By the end of this article, you will be able to identify the piece three specific common financial problems and learn to avoid them in your life.

The first issue we all face is delaying saving money in our 401(k) for retirement. You can even put money away in a savings account or 401(k), either is fine. The moral of the story is that many people fail to start saving for retirement from an early age. If you ask someone when they want to retire, the most common answer is at the latest by their mid-60s. You will then ask the same person how much they have set aside for retirement and find out it is not sufficient to do so.

Many people have not even sat down to plan how much they need to save on an annual basis in order to retire by their goal. Do not make this mistake, start planning today how much you need to put away and do it.

The second problem we all face every day is learning not to fall victim to financial sales pitches. Everywhere you turn there is someone or something advertising on the TV, radio, or Internet about promising great returns. Billions of dollars is spent on marketing by financial institutions every year. These commercials are meant to grab your attention and attached to your emotional being. A rule of thumb here is to stay clear of people who pressure you to make decisions. Also stay clear of people who promise high returns. If you do meet someone who promises high returns, you need to invest and see if they have had the proper training and experience to help you.

The third thing that we all do not do is spend time doing due diligence before we purchase or make an investment. You must shop around and read some reviews about different investments and different investment firms before taking action. Checking track records and getting references from people you are considering doing business with is a must. There is a lot of different homework to be done and much of it can be overwhelming to the average person. You must take some time and learn to do this homework and ask the proper questions that are needed before you invest or make big commitments and purchases.

How to Fix Your Financial Problems

No, this is not a comprehensive course on magically repairing your finances. All we are going to do is encourage you to take a look at your financial situation right now and make some realistic decisions. Everything we discuss on this blog is put in the context of building a better life for yourself and your loved ones. So what we are going to do here is simply examine where you are financially, how you got there and some essential things you need to do to gradually get to your ideal financial life. You understand (or should understand) that you need to know where you want to go to be able to plot a course to any destination. The same holds true for financial planning. Today, we shall temporarily ignore our financial problems and devise a strategy for creating a healthy financial life.

Here are some vital things you need to do to begin improving your financial life.

1. Dedicate a notebook for your financial planning and development. If you prefer a computerized system, use any computerized accounting system with which you are most comfortable. The key is to review your plan each week. You must become actively involved in resolving your financial condition.

2. Broadly write down where you would like to be financially in the next 5 years. Your statement should be something like this: "Today is (date). On (date 5 years from today) I will be free from the following debts: (list debts you want paid). I will also have financial investments (or savings) totaling ($amount)." It is not necessary that your statement predicts you to be totally debt-free. It simply needs to vocalize the items you want to be rid of within a five year period. The idea here is to get your mind working on applying your income in specific ways to improve your financial health.

3. Write down the total amount of money you currently receive each month. This amount is what you have to

use to pay off your monthly debt obligations and to invest in your savings program at this time. For some of us, this figure may appear woefully inadequate to fund our plans and meet our current obligations. Do not despair! Remember, we are working with a 5-year development plan. We will change our financial circumstances, as we go along, to improve our chances of realizing our financial goals. This is absolutely do-able!

4. Calculate the total amount of money remaining each month after paying your due obligations. Due obligations also include the costs of getting to work.

5. From this money, deduct a portion for savings investment. YOU MUST DO THIS! This portion must be relative to what you can truly afford at this time. The shortfall towards your ideal savings investment will be made up at a later time. The idea here is to work on all aspects of your financial plan. Put this amount into a savings account until it grows large enough to open an investment account such as a mutual fund. If you have financial perks on your job, such as a 401k plan, use it instead. You want this money to become as untouchable as you can make it.

6. Adjust your current living habits to suit your current financial abilities. Yes, you may have to make some temporary entertainment sacrifices and control your instant gratification urges, but this is only temporary. Develop some self-control regarding your impulse spending. Remember that you are committing yourself to change your financial life in just 5 years. You can do this. Psychologists will confirm that it takes as little as 30 days of consistent behavior to change a habit. The money you will invest in your savings will come mainly from your entertainment budget (or lack thereof). Most people do not realize this, but poor financial health is largely a matter of bad spending habits. They spend more in entertainment than they can really afford. One 50-cent bag of chips daily = $15 per month = $180 per year. This is $180 that could have been invested in your savings program. Do the math with your impulse spending, then decide if it's worth keeping the habit.

7. Sort your bills by the size of the balances. Pay only the bare minimum on each bill, except the smallest one. Pick the smallest balance and begin to pay it down. Whenever you can, without sacrificing your savings

program, pay something extra on that bill. Even $1.00 makes a huge difference over time. Wherever possible, stipulate that the extra money be applied to the principal amount owed. Make your payments on time, as much as possible. This will reduce added costs such as penalty fees, increased interest rates, etc. When that balance is paid off, add that payment amount to the next smallest bill in line and do the same. Continue this process until all your unwanted bills are paid off. Do not stop until all your bills are wiped out.

8. Every week, without fail, review your financial plan and make any positive adjustments you can. Post your written plan on your bedroom wall, in your office or anywhere in your home where you can easily see it daily! Post your savings progress, too. You want to see that you are progressing. Post the current bill you are paying down and how soon it will be paid off according to your schedule. Go to war on those bills while developing a strategy for increasing your savings investment. Never forget your savings investment. That money is the only money that you will keep from your earnings. Love it and honor it and do whatever you can to increase it. Get a part-time job, if necessary, and use

that income solely for increasing your savings investment.

Words of caution

As previously mentioned, this plan is not comprehensive. It is designed to give you a practical starting point to help you dig yourself out of whatever financial hole you currently perceive yourself to be in. This plan works only for those who work it patiently. Five years appears to be a long time, but in reality we are only talking about 1825 days! Your greatest enemy during this time will be your uncontrolled bad spending habits. Do not lose patience with your progress. Despair is a product of impatience! Impatience makes you do irrational things, such as gambling with your investment program. State Lotteries may hold the promise of forever solving all your financial problems. By all means, you may discreetly invest a dollar or two this way, but do not become dependent on gambling (in any form) as an investment program. When you decide that you are able to take risks to increase your savings investments, you should learn all you can about financial trading and investments. There are many reputable places from which you can receive this essential information to enable you to make informed decisions. If you are at the point where you are considering investing, the following links will take you to sites that may be able to help you. As usual, perform due diligence before investing money in any enterprise.

How to Solve Financial Problems in Personal Life

Life is full of challenges and lessons. Among all challenges or problems, financial problem fares one in the top. If you happened to be in the midst of troubling personal financial issue, it is extremely difficult to think and focus on anything else in your life. Unless you start addressing the issues with utmost urgency, trust that it would be long before you extricate yourself from the predicament of your life. There is no way but face your fears squarely and deal with it with discipline and precision. The writer has kept his focus on issues related persons challenged with heavy debt, nevertheless, others may also get benefited by the guidelines outlined here.

Fortunately, there are more than one ways to handle your troubling financial situation.

Nevertheless, you must keep in mind that you need to change your lifestyles dramatically if you ever want to come out of your debt hole. If you are not ready for sacrifices and changes in your life, then everything else you try is meaningless. For those who are willing to change, firstly, it is important to understand that you cannot live a lifestyle that you cannot support financially. Second, you cannot live a lifestyle just to impress others even while you are sinking deeper. Decide to put a full stop for all those tendencies and live a life that can help you to overcome your troubles.

Stop all unnecessary expenditures with immediate effect.

Discuss with your spouse, if married, and take his/her feedback on areas of cost cutting. Limiting or ending certain expenditures can save you money. Indeed, there could be many hidden recurring costs that you keep paying month after month.

Over a period, if you are not watchful of our monthly bills, the small recurring expenses add up substantially. Carefully go through all periodic statements and take action to stop the recurring payments that are not adding value to your life.

Go through the following action list, and implement most of them as soon as possible,

1. Change your mobile plan to reduce the overall monthly bill. Limit the mobile phone usage only when necessary. Avoid gossiping on mobile phone! If possible change your billing plan from post paid to prepaid!

2. Same goes to your broadband/mobile internet connection. Have a cheaper broadband plan. Find out what else you can settle for, if you cannot find cheaper alternatives.

3. Start reducing the power consumption by limited use of electrical appliances such as air conditioner, heater etc wherever possible. However, do not make you shiver or cook yourself in heat. Be discerning.

4. Reduce water consumption at home. For some it may sound silly. However, in some parts of the world, water is expensive and limited. See if reducing water usage makes sense in your case.

5. Consolidate your grocery purchases and buy from discount retail stores. Try to find discount coupons wherever available. You will be surprised how much you can save.

6. Stop expensive magazine subscriptions at home for time being. Over a period we would have subscribed expensive magazines. Stop most, if not all, if you can.

7. Start using pubic transport wherever and whenever possible instead of using taxi or own car. In some countries, pooling of car is encouraged. See if you can find car pooling in your neighborhood.

8. Walk down to nearest store instead of using your car if you want to buy groceries. Walking is a good exercise and helps you to have fresh air!

9. Stop alcohol consumption and smoking, and STOP Gambling, if you are into it. All these habits only aggravate your situation, not alleviate.

10. Stop borrowing from credit cards and put away all credit cards in your closet/drawer. Start negotiating with credit card companies or banks by conveying them that you want to close your credit cards. Banks would

offer you monthly fixed payment plans and the advantage is all the stinging monthly interest would be stopped piling up on your credit. However, you should be prompt in paying monthly fixed payments. It is better if you can find a community center that offers free financial advice for debt consolidation, for example. If possible take guidance from a financial advisor regarding ways to manage your risky situation.

11. Aggressively go through your monthly bills and see areas for reduction or elimination

12. If you are paying to high rent for your home, relocate to a cheaper residence without compromising on your family safety. If you are still single you may decide to share accommodation with any of your friends or colleagues. Since rent can be substantial part of your monthly expenses, you may move to live with your parents or relatives temporarily, if feasible. Nevertheless, you need to talk to your family first before taking your decision.

13. If you are paying higher mortgage interest, try to refinance at a cheaper interest rate.

14. If your children are using mobile phones, you may decide to terminate those mobile plans temporarily.

15. If you and your family are regularly eating in restaurants, put stop to it and eat at home. If you are working outside, you may even think of carrying food, like sandwiches, from home for lunch. This should apply to everyone in the family.

16. If practical, stop using laundry service and wash and press your cloths at home. Remember self-help is the best help.

17. Try to get whatever support you can get from your friends and colleagues to generate ideas to earn extra cash for you. You will be surprised to find our some very practical ideas generated by brainstorming with others.

All the above steps need preparation, determination, and discipline on your part and your family. All of your family members should understand why the cost cutting measures are being done because their co-operation is absolutely essential. Encourage your family members to come out with ideas to help the cost cutting project. Even give a name to your project. Create a goal for your initiative. Get your family involvement. If you consistently follow your debt clearing plan or project, soon you will find smile on your face. Wait no more and act today. Make your days brighter minus the look of worries on your face. Because, you deserved to be happy, let your past mistakes not haunt your forever.

Finally, the guidelines outlined above are not exhaustive and does not cover all plausible conditions. Therefore, if you find this list incomplete, you may seek a professional help in your area. A professional not only helps you to gain confidence and enables you to get out of your predicament.

www.ingramcontent.com/pod-product-compliance
Lightning Source LLC
Chambersburg PA
CBHW070522220526
45467CB00002B/806